Squire Surname

Ireland: 1600s to 1900s

From Ireland Church Records of Baptism, Marriage and Death

Comprised of Roman Catholic and Church of Ireland Records

From Counties Carlow, Cork, Kerry and Dublin City

Compiled by **Donovan Hurst**

April 23, 2013

ISBN: 1939958210
ISBN-13: 978-1-939958-21-1

Dedication

This work is dedicated to all of those that came before us and shaped our lives to make us the people that we are today.

Table of Contents

Introduction

This is a compilation of individuals who have the surname of Squire that lived in the country of Ireland from the 1600s to the 1900s. I have placed each entry into one of four categories: Families, Individual Births/Baptisms, Individual Burials, and Individual Marriages. If a marriage entry primarily concerns an Individual Squire whom is female, then I have placed that entry under the category of Individual Marriages. If a marriage entry primarily concerns an Individual Squire whom is male, then I have placed that entry under the category of Families. Images of many of these listings are available at http://churchrecords.irishgenealogy.ie/churchrecords/.

To help guide the reader of this work, the format of this book is as follows:

- Main Family Entry (Husband and Wife) (Father and Mother)

  o Child of Main Family Entry, including Spouse(s) when available

    ▪ Grandchild of Main Family Entry, including Spouse(s) when available

    • Great-Grandchild of Main Family Entry, including Spouse(s) when available

(Bolded Text) following any entry includes any additional information such as Residence(s), Occupation(s), Signature(s), etc. when available.

Hurst

Some of the fonts used in this work symbolizes Celtic writing. The traditional letters, numbers, and punctuation marks and their Celtic counterparts are as follows:

Traditional Letters (Uppercase & Lowercase)

A a B b C c D d E f G g H h I i J j K k L l M m N n O o P p Q q R r S s T t U u V v W w X x Y y Z z

Celtic Letters (Uppercase & Lowercase)

A a B b C c D ð E e F ꝼ G g H h I í J j K k L l M m

N n O o P p Q q R ʀ S s T t U u V ʋ W ꝏ X x Y y Z z

Traditional Numbers

1 2 3 4 5 6 7 8 9 10

Celtic Numbers

1 2 3 4 5 6 7 8 9 10

Traditional Punctuation

. , : ' " & - ( )

Celtic Punctuation

. , : ' " & - ( )

Parish Churches

Carlow (Church of Ireland)

Aghold Parish.

Cork & Ross

(Roman Catholic or RC)

Cork - SS. Peter & Paul Parish and Kinsale Parish.

Dublin (Church of Ireland)

Irishtown Parish, Leeson Park Parish, Rathmines Parish, St. Andrew Parish, St. Catherine Parish, St. James Parish, St. Luke Parish, St. Mark Parish, St. Mary Parish, St. Nicholas Within Parish, St. Nicholas Without Parish, St. Paul Parish, St. Peter Parish, and Taney Parish.

Families

- Edward Squire, bur. 18 May 1705 (Burial, **St. John Parish**) & Avis Jane Squire

  - Jane Squire – b. 24 Nov 1694, bapt. 27 Nov 1694 (Baptism, **St. John Parish**)

  - John Squire – b. 28 Jan 1699, bapt. 29 Jan 1699 (Baptism, **St. John Parish**), bur. 24 Apr 1700 (Burial, **St. John Parish**)

  - Mary Squire – b. 2 Feb 1704, bapt. 6 Feb 1704 (Baptism, **St. John Parish**)

Edward Squire (father):

Residence - Fishamble Street - January 29, 1699

February 6, 1704

Occupation - Tailor - January 18, 1699

February 6, 1704

- Edward Squire & Sabina Brothera – 23 Aug 1708 (Marriage, **St. Nicholas Without Parish**)

Edward Squire (husband):

Residence - St. Nicholas Without Parish - August 23, 1708

Sabina Brothera (wife):

Residence - St. Nicholas Without Parish - August 23, 1708

Hurst

- Frederick Squire & Mary Helen Squire

  - Archibald William Squire – b. 27 Dec 1877, bapt. 13 Mar 1878 (Baptism, **Leeson Park Parish**)

Frederick Squire (father):

Residence - Curragh Camp - March 13, 1878

Occupation - Captain, 93rd Highlander - March 13, 1878

- John Squire & Eleanor Squire

  - Anne Squire – bapt. 11 Sep 1741 (Baptism, **St. Luke Parish**)

- John Squire & Eleanor Unknown

  - Elizabeth Squire – bapt. 15 Jan 1737 (Baptism, **St. Nicholas Without Parish**)

John Squire (father):

Residence - Plunkett Street - January 15, 1737

- John Squire & Ellen Hingston

  - John Squire – bapt. 14 Mar 1855 (Baptism, **Cork - SS. Peter & Paul Parish (RC)**)

- John Squire & Frances Squire

  - John Squire – bapt. 14 Jun 1726 (Baptism, **St. Catherine Parish**)

- John Squire & Jane Unknown

  - Jane Squire – bapt. 27 Apr 1711 (Baptism, **St. Nicholas Without Parish**)

John Squire (father):

Residence - Plunkett Street - April 27, 1711

Squire Surname Ireland: 1600s to 1900s

- John Squire & Unknown

  o Stephen Squire – bapt. 26 Jul 1702 (Baptism, **St. Nicholas Within Parish**)

- Pierre William Henry Squire & Henrietta Elizabeth Squire

  o Sarah Catherine Squire – b. 1 Nov 1858, bapt. 21 Nov 1858 (Baptism, **Rathmines Parish**)

  o Henrietta Elizabeth Squire – b. 9 Sep 1860, bapt. 19 Dec 1860 (Baptism, **St. Peter Parish**)

Pierre William Henry Squire (father):

Residence - 58 Rathmines Road - November 21, 1858

2 Grosvenor Road, Rathgar - December 19, 1860

Occupation - Wine Merchant - November 21, 1858

Merchant - December 19, 1860

- Richard Squire & Unknown

  o Samuel Squire – bapt. 24 Jan 1690 (Baptism, **St. John Parish**)

- Samuel Squire & Mary Squire

  o Mary Squire – b. 26 Mar 1897, bapt. 11 Apr 1897 (Baptism, **St. Catherine Parish**)

  o George Squire – b. 5 Jun 1899, bapt. 22 Jun 1899 (Baptism, **St. Peter Parish**)

Samuel Squire (father):

Residence - 14 Reginald Square - April 11, 1897

1 Glover's Alley - June 22, 1899

Occupation - Hop Bitter Brewer - April 11, 1897

Brewer - June 22, 1899

3

Hurst

- Steward Squire & Susanna Unknown

  o Anne Squire – bapt. 16 Jul 1758 (Baptism, **St. Catherine Parish**)

  o Stephen Squire – bapt. 16 Nov 1766 (Baptism, **St. James Parish**)

  o John Squire – bapt. 18 Dec 1768 (Baptism, **St. James Parish**)

Steward Squire (father):

Occupation - Shoe Maker - November 16, 1766

December 18, 1768

- William Squire & Margaret Nolan

  o Jane Squire – bapt. 13 Apr 1829 (Baptism, **Kinsale Parish (RC)**)

William Squire (father):

Residence - Cove - April 13, 1829

- William Squire, bur. 15 Nov 1709 (Burial, **St. Mary Parish**) & Unknown

  o William Squire – bur. 5 Feb 1710 (Burial, **St. Mary Parish**)

William Squire (father):

Occupation - Merchant - before November 15, 1709

- William Henry Squire & Henrietta Elizabeth Squire

  o Henry William Squire – b. 28 Sep 1870, bapt. 8 Oct 1870 (Baptism, **Irishtown Parish**)

  o William Henry Squire – b. 28 Sep 1870, bapt. 8 Oct 1870 (Baptism, **Irishtown Parish**)

  o Avis Emma Squire – b. 10 Nov 1871, bapt. 7 Jul 1872 (Baptism, **St. Mark Parish**)

  o Laura Georgina Squire – b. 18 Jun 1873, bapt. 20 Aug 1873 (Baptism, **St. Mark Parish**)

Squire Surname Ireland: 1600s to 1900s

William Henny Squine (father):

Residence - Irishtown - October 8, 1870

Great Brunswick Street - July 7, 1872

30 Lombard Street - August 20, 1873

Occupation - Traveller - October 8, 1870

Caretaker to Concert Room - July 7, 1872

Steward - August 20, 1873

Individual Baptisms/Births

None Were Listed

Individual Burials

- Anne Squire – bur. 9 Feb 1641 (Burial, **St. John Parish**)

- Catherine Squire – bur. 9 Feb 1720 (Burial, **St. Mary Parish**)

- Catherine Squire – bur. Unclear April Unclear (Burial, **Aghold Parish**)

Catherine Squire (deceased):

Residence - Aghold - before April Unclear, Unclear

Remarks about Burial - The page of the church register is missing the

day and year of Catherine Squire's burial.

- Edward Squire – bur. 13 Mar 1725 (Burial, **St. Nicholas Without Parish**)

Edward Squire (deceased):

Residence - Patrick Street - March 13, 1725

- Elizabeth Squire – b. 1896, bur. 28 Apr 1897 (Burial, **Taney Parish**)

Elizabeth Squire (deceased):

Residence - Dundrum - before April 28, 1897

Age at Death - 1 year

Hurst

- James Squire – bur. 5 Aug 1640 (Burial, **St. John Parish**)

- Jane Squire – bur. 1 Aug 1711 (Burial, **St. Nicholas Without Parish**)

Jane Squire (deceased):

   Residence - New Row - before August 1, 1711

- John Squire – bur. 1 May 1625 (Burial, **St. John Parish**)

John Squire (deceased):

   Occupation - Sexton of this Church - May 1, 1625

- John Squire – bur. 29 Feb 1720 (Burial, **St. Nicholas Without Parish**)

John Squire (deceased):

   Residence - Plunkett Street - before February 29, 1720

- John Squire – bur. 18 Sep 1729 (Burial, **St. Catherine Parish**)

John Squire (deceased):

   Age at Death - child

- Mary Squire – bur. 9 Feb 1746 (Burial, **St. Paul Parish**)

- Peter Squire – bur. Aug 1710 (Burial, **St. Nicholas Without Parish**)

Peter Squire (deceased):

   Residence - The Coombe - before August 1710

Squire Surname Ireland: 1600s to 1900s

- Susanna Squire – bur. 14 Sep 1714 (Burial, **St. Nicholus Without Parish**)

Susanna Squire (deceased):

 Residence - Plunkett Street - before September 14, 1714

- Thomas Squire – bur. 9 Nov 1761 (Burial, **St. Paul Parish**)

Thomas Squire (deceased):

 Occupation - Reverend - before November 9, 1761

- Unknown Squire – bur. 8 Feb 1712 (Burial, **St. Nicholas Without Parish**)

Unknown Squire (deceased):

 Residence - Swift's Alley - before February 8, 1712

- Unknown Squire – bur. 26 Mar 1746 (Burial, **St. Nicholas Without Parish**)

Unknown Squire (deceased):

 Residence - Coombe - before March 26, 1746

- Unknown Squire – b. 1768, bur. 30 Jan 1779 (Burial, **St. Nicholas Without Parish**)

Unknown Squire (deceased):

 Residence - Patrick Street - before January 30, 1779

 Age at Death - 11 years

Hurst

- William Squire – bur. 15 Apr 1713 (Burial, **St. Paul Parish**)

- William Squire – bur. 30 Nov 1713 (Burial, **St. Paul Parish**)

- William Squire – bur. 10 Jul 1721 (Burial, **St. Nicholas Without Parish**)

William Squire (deceased):

Residence - Bride's Alley - before July 10, 1721

Individual Marriages

- Debora Squire & John Bareley – 6 Nov 1732 (Marriage, **St. Catherine Parish**)

- Lilia Squire & Henry Caddow – 17 Feb 1726 (Marriage, **St. Andrew Parish**)

- Mary Squire & Richard Barnwell (B a r n w e l l) – 9 Jul 1730 (Marriage, **St. Andrew Parish**)

- Sabina Squire & John Quinn – 11 Apr 1723 (Marriage, **St. Nicholas Without Parish**)

- Susanna Squire & George Dodson – 9 Jul 1730 (Marriage, **St. Andrew Parish**)

Name Variations

Includes Latin and Abbreviated forms of names found in the original documents.

Abigail = Abigale, Abigall

Anne = Ann, Anna, Annae

Bartholomew = Barth, Bartholmeus, Bartholomeo

Bridget = Birgis, Brigid, Brigida, Bridgit

Catherine = Catharine, Catharina, Catharinae, Catherina, Cath, Catha, Cathae, Cathe, Cathn, Kate

Charles = Carolus, Charls, Chas

Christopher = Christoph

Daniel = Danielem, Danielis

Edmund = Edmond

Edward = Ed, Edwd

Eleanor = Eleo, Eleonora, Elinor, Ellenor

Elizabeth = Betty, Elisa, Elisabeth, Eliz, Eliza, Elizab, Elizh, Elizth

Ellen = Elena, Ellena

Emily = Emilia

Esther = Essie, Ester

Francis = Fransicum

George = Geo, Georg, Georgius

Grace = Gratiae

Gulielmo = Guil, Guillelmi, Gulielmum, Guillelmus, Gulmi

Helen = Helena

Squire Surname Ireland: 1600s to 1900s

Honor = Hanora, Honora

James = Jacobi, Jacobus, Jas

Jane = Joanna

Jeanne = Jeannae, Joannae

Joan = Johanna, Joney

John = Jno, Joannem, Joannes, Johannis

Joseph = Jos

Juliana = Julian

Leticia = Letitia, Lettice, Letticia

Lewis = Louis

Luke = Lucas

Margaret = Margarita, Margaritae, Margeret, Marget, Margt

Martha = Marthae

Mary = Maria, My

Mary Anne = Marianna, Marianne, Maryanne

Michael = Michaelis, Michl

Patrick = Pat, Patt, Patk, Patricii, Patricius

Peter = Petri

Richard = Ricardi, Ricardus, Rich, Richd

Robert = Roberti

Rose = Rosa, Rosae

Thomas = Thom, Thomae, Thoms, Thos, Ths

Timothy = Timotheus, Timy

William = Wil, Will, Willm, Wm

Notes

Notes

Notes

Notes

Notes

Notes

Index

Hurst

U

About The Author

Donovan Hurst graduated from San Diego State University with a Bachelor of Arts in the major field of studies of History and a minor in the field of studies of Anthropology. He is a current member of The General Society of Mayflower Descendants and has been conducting genealogical research for over 10 years tracing back his ancestors to their ancestral homelands in Denmark, England, France, Germany, Ireland, Norway, and Scotland.

www.ingramcontent.com/pod-product-compliance
Lightning Source LLC
Chambersburg PA
CBHW080058280326
41934CB00014B/3357